# Time and Song of the River Man

John Onyeche

Phoenix Voices Publishing

Copyright © 2023 by John Chinaka Onyeche

All rights reserved. No part of this publication may be reproduced, stored or transmitted in any form or by any means, electronic, mechanical, photocopying, recording, scanning, or otherwise without written permission from the publisher. It is illegal to copy this book, post it to a website, or distribute it by any other means without permission.

This novel is entirely a work of fiction. The names, characters and incidents portrayed in it are the work of the author's imagination. Any resemblance to actual persons, living or dead, events or localities is entirely coincidental.

John Chinaka Onyeche asserts the moral right to be identified as the author of this work.

John Chinaka Onyeche has no responsibility for the persistence or accuracy of URLs for external or third-party Internet Websites referred to in this publication and does not guarantee that any content on such Websites is, or will remain, accurate or appropriate.

*Designations used by companies to distinguish their products are often claimed as trademarks. All brand names and product names used in this book and on its cover are trade names, service marks, trademarks and registered trademarks of their respective owners. The publishers and the book are not associated with any product or vendor mentioned in this book. None of the companies referenced within the book have endorsed the book.*

# **Contents**


Message From the Author     1

Foreword     2

1. Wandering and a Wanderer     4

2. We Are All Fishermen with Broken Nets     6

3. At the Riverbank     8

4. Home Alone     9

5. Home Calls     11

6. Cathari (pure ones)     13

7. Words Tracked on the Wood     14

8. Journeying     15

9. Silent Nights     16

10. Sleepless Nights     17

11. Words     18

12. For Gift Ugochi     19

13. Gift is Dead     20

14. For the Boys Who Left Home     21

15. Funeral of Things We Lost     23

16. Naming of Grief     24

17. Realities of Our Being     25

18. Nameless     26

19. Things that Happened to Us     27

20. Sermon for the Once Loved     28

21. When You Have None to Cheer You Up     29

22. Is There No Time to Say Goodbyes?     31

23. Gin and Ship     33

24. Our Tales     34

25. There is a Place Where I Belong     35

26. How We Prayed Knowing Our Roots     37

27. History     38

28. Slavery     40

29. Water Act     41

30. The Lad and the River     42

31. Sowing Time     44

32. The Place of Gods     45

33. About Last Night     47

34. Watching the River Flow     49

35. Motherhood     51

36. Conversation with the Ghost of My Mother After My Wife Left Home Why Our Kids     53

37. Marriage 1     55

38. Marriage 2 — 56

39. Titillation (Don't Blame Me) — 57

40. My Woman — 59

41. A Requiem — 61

42. First Night in the City of My Father — 62

43. For My Son (Sobeife) — 64

44. Heaven is Not Safe — 66

45. Is God a Poet (Joel) — 68

46. Sermon One — 69

47. Begging Brother — 70

48. Painter — 71

49. Songs — 72

50. Broken Muse — 73

51. Season of Songs — 74

52. Surge — 75

53. Singing Distance — 76

54. Stitching Memories — 77

55. Orchestra of Existence — 78

56. Staring at Self in a Portrait of Time — 79

57. Time and Songs — 81

58. Song One — 82

59. The First Time I Singed — 84

60. We all Sing — 85

61. After a Birth — 86

62. Sowing Time     87

63. Time     88

64. Good Night     89

65. Self at the 33rd Bridge     90

66. Two-Timing     92

67. Hope     93

About the Author     94

# Message From the Author

At the funeral of the things we lost The preacher presented us with sermons on life after death
Amen becomes the soothing ointment we rubbed our broken hearts until it heals their wounds
This is another way of hiding that we are broken
That death of one is the death of all If not, why do you echo amen to hide away from the sting of death? —John Chinaka Onyeche
Of whatever becomes this lad, know that I will swim across the tide and time, if the river wants me or
never,
#BrokenBoysMuse

# Foreword

Onyeche's Time and Songs of the River Men, is a lyrical journey through the heart's deepest echoes. Here, grief and love intertwine, painted with hauntingly beautiful language that flows like a timeless river, carrying the reader to the shores of profound emotion.

- **Jeff Iwu**, Author, Verdict of the Gods.

In "Time and Songs of the River Men", John Onyeche's poetry takes an amazing stylistic shift both in form and in content as he echoes the graveside canticles of his homeland, (the land of fishermen with broken nets). This shift is sure to ignite sheer curiosity and zest in any assiduous reader of Onyeche's works. As a burden writer "voicing the grief that dwells within" Onyeche employs figures of sounds and heart-melting metaphors that wail for a homeland marred by despair that mourns for the impoverished lives and the man-made hell that flows in the land, river, mind and heart of his region.

This book, is multifaceted, deep, thought provoking and educative, well loaded with life experiences; of love, romance, pain, marriage, dreams and desires that sets the bard's ink sailing. I strongly recommend this book to you; lovers of wisdom and humanity.

— **Samuel Onyeche.**

African writer; author of Songs of My Country.

Time & song of the River Men, is a chronicle of grief, loss, the unknown and hope all interconnected like a river meandering into each other through the tides of metaphors and requiem until you finally set sail on the banks of gratification.

Onyeche's chapbook is as compelling & soothing as the lush tranquility of a river, each poem written with lucid flourish. This is a must-read for all lovers of beautiful and lyrical poetry. - **Solomon Timothy Hamza-King**

This poetry collection by John Chinaka Onyeche defines the title of the poems well, yet taking the freedom route to expression. A majestic ride through the crafty use of words offers a solace to the lost souls. Onyeche is filled with talent of mind and heart.

-**Sushant Thapa**, Nepal. (Author of poetry collection "Love's Cradle," World Inkers Printing and Publishing, New York, USA and Dakar, Senegal, Africa)

Time & song of the River Men, is a trip down memory lane and a present day-dream. Onyeche's chapbook travels through time to tell us of loss, pain and grief. His language like slow dripping water reads with a lyrical beauty that makes you forget the message to forget yourself in its beauty.

"Bare I arrive, Clad as I depart" the poet sings and we are reminded of the reality of our being and un-being. We wish at the time that we can truly go beyond the words of this poet into his emotions as the journey progresses. We lull our canoes and just listen because John is weaving more than words. - **Abasiama Udom**, Editor, Stripes Literary Magazine

vii

# Wandering and a Wanderer

This realm is not ours the preacher softly sighed,

Yet I claim my departure the day I am untying my pace.

Is there beauty in death's embrace?

As I tread the path leaving this home,

Entering realms fairytale or satire,

A journey guided by an unseen harp.

Slow strides, swift steps, the pace may wane,

Knowing self's truth - boundaries to gain.

At life's farthest edge I lay my form,

My name on tongues, yet distant and shabby.

Souls notice the void, where life's breath departs,

In death's empire, do we find arts beautiful?

The preacher raised a hand affirmed the grace,

Heaven, he invoked as tears left a trace within,

Time & Song of the River Man

For this world is not our true dwelling,

We gathered strength in unity as hearts intertwined.

If heaven is a metaphor, how is your usage shown?
The door to the last home a grave's known,
Where both great and humble, side by side reside,
In the address of eternity, they peacefully stay.

# We Are All Fishermen with Broken Nets

If foresight had whispered catch fleeing from the net,
Last night repairs, we would have mended every tear.
Watermen arrived ventured into the deep,
Fishes heard our calls in formation they had dive.
In unity they queued asking for a grand score,
But a net cracked and unprepared is no extra.
For a grand catch requires a net well-tended,
Yet we cast with flaws our hopes unblending.
You the river embraced us on the boat's nod,
Guiding us through night's slumber showing us how,
To seek what is elusive yet find what is true,
Your presence in our hearts is a dance of sorts.
Are you still beside us or have you sailed away?
Joining tales of watermen's ships a different haven,
Where catches are bounteous nets remain whole,

Where fish are not lost where destinies unfurl.

We tried our best your life within our grasp,

But hardness prevailed your gasp for life clutched,

Like fish your breath in water a fleeting act,

As you left the world a space in between.

Are we like air when life's journeys thru?

Perhaps like whispers our essence is rolled,

Eternal unseen a presence in every flurry,

A memory's echo - a heart's cherished faith.

# At the Riverbank

No epistle bears words to inscribe for you,
Dearest boy-child, embark upon life's voyage,
Flow akin to a river, coursing diverse realms,
Manifesting destinies, significance, and essence.
Both the envisioned and the unforeseen,
Extend their hands, like reeds by the banks,
Wherein we shed our dreams each day,
Undergo renewal, bathing hope anew,
Within the vast ocean and realm of words.

# Home Alone

Should this path not guide survival,
Within the confines of a solitary dwelling,
After shedding tears that veil my form,
Concealing within these walls, my very being,
Within this abode of stone-laden memories,
Where once the world cast its gaze upon me,
First a boy, and later, a man,
Moistened by the morning's tender dew,
A garment woven without the thread of desolation,
As a wanderer, retracing steps to the origin,
Encountering time's enigmatic presence,
It queries, "Where does this river find its source?"
While a whispered response echoes, carry home,
Within you, the remnants of history's tapestry,
Fuse them to the fragments of the present,
Learning to subsist where existence resembles mist,
Never barter away your mantle under the sun's embrace,
Home Alone
If this, indeed, denotes survival within solitude,

Embrace the art of allowing life to gleam in its course,
To radiate within its natural flow and glow."

# Home Calls

In the village's assembly, a gathering profound,
Elders brought forth kola-nuts, blessings open,
Split into seven, each piece a wish,
For good days ahead, a destiny to prize.
Aboard ships into destiny we set sail,
Praying never to forget home's anecdote,
Promising to return city-like, to build anew,
But we sailed to a new world, unsure, awry.
Not as slaves, yet not fully free,
The ship's journey held uncertainty,
Homeland grew distant, fear took grip,
The path back, once welcoming, now turned cold.
We desired never to return,
Home transformed, our hearts shuddering,
Now home is where we write, a distant place,
Home Calls
The sea echoes our voyage, its rhythmic hug.
Once we called home an anchor, so sure,
Voices rang strong, a message to stomach,
Labeling those who left as feeble hearts,

Now home is submerged beneath waters' sculptures.

When home beckons, death's shadow looms,

Yet, what is home if we flee its places?

A paradox this yearning we have branded,

For home, our anchor, still calls us to its own.

# Cathari (pure ones)

Daily we split our hearts wide-ranging,

Seeking lassos, seeking where holes reside.

Life devoid of introspection's stare,

Fear's whispers echo, abhorrence's vapor.

Ego ascends to heart's ruling seat,

In pursuit of those deemed evil alone.

Seven evils enter as our hearts fragment,

Upon the altar of a nation's beating core.

Who kills to claim righteousness' guise?

Mend not just wounds, but the soul's bonds.

Until we stand distant truth embraced,

Before the sun's rays, in every interstellar.

Cathari (pure ones)

Seek not to mask in righteous masquerade,

Daily, unseat ego that contests.

Let introspection mend the ego's throne,

Unifying hearts as understanding's given away.

# Words Tracked on the Wood

Night's edges torn apart as if by fate's arrow,

Words hammered like nails, a gong's command,

Echoing betrayal, echoing countless ages,

Actions against the thatched roof's weeping.

In a rainy night splattered with cheetah's hue,

I lay bare abandoned my shelter cock-eyed,

My heart like fallow land barren and dry,

Words pour forth gone with a moan.

River-like words spill; villages rub out,

Our streams overflow past embraced,

Once-celebrated abode's whispers now imply,

"Seek elsewhere leave this place, don't refute."

# Journeying

Beside the shore, as darkness embraced the night,
Our vessel found haven, its journey complete,
We poured forth our yearnings to the river's care,
For it to bear away the weight of our hopes,
To reveal the traveler's essence, we embody.
As the night belongs to vigilant sentinels,
And the morn to the laborer's toil,
Here, within these echoing bounds, lend your voice,
Surrender your essence to the river's embrace,
There, perhaps, your tears will be carried away,
Vanishing along with the path that lies ahead,
Both the process of becoming and unbecoming,
As the figure on the ship's deck sighs, "Alas!"
Understand, this is not composed in verse,
But a heartfelt reflection upon the shores of existence.

# Silent Nights

The silence thickened,
Within the verdant woods,
Where owls serenade, Hoot, hoot, hoot.
No nightingale's sweet song,
No lullabies to cradle us,
No infant's laughter to greet the night,
Hoot, hoot, hoot.
The darkness reverberated,
Grief settled like an anchor,
Where once we aimed for the stars,
In their celestial wanderings,
Hoot, hoot, hoot.
Silent Nights
Now the dirge has arrived,
No melody lingers on our tongues,
As silent nights stretch endlessly.

# Sleepless Nights

My hands clasp the phone with fervor,

My thoughts race like Formula One autos,

Fingers dance, translating the heart's rhythm,

As it unfolds to embrace the deluge of inspiration—

Yet, my eyes dangle in the realm of dreams,

I chase countless phrases, a tireless pursuit,

To ensure my heart finds the tranquil brooks,

Where stillness adorns itself in robes of peace.

I pledge my heart's limbs to the bed,

Countless thoughts drench me in waves,

A labyrinth of time slips through my grasp,

A web of dreams, yet to take tangible form.

A kiss shared across the keys,

A night devoid of slumber, I ponder,

Do we all harbor a dream or fragment,

Sleepless Nights

That keeps us wide-eyed in contemplation?

# Words

Once more under the moon's tender watch,
I find myself drawn back to this sacred space,
To weave language onto the tapestry of your wound -
Should you unearth solace amidst these verses,
Immerse your heart in their sanctifying waters,
Into liberated pathways and unburdened trails.
*O wanderer of the land!*
If I, a mere specter ceases to tread here again
Embark upon the route toward tombs,
Resurrect these lines from the depths of me,
Anoint your aching heart with their essence.
Until the dawn's embrace graces the sky,
Acknowledge that words possess a redemptive cadence,
Steal them away to mend where scars have settled,
Words
For with the morning's advent,
Words, too, carry the promise of deliverance,
Seize them where the scars persist.

# For Gift Ugochi

With pen in hand, I inscribe you upon the waters,
Your ship's early departure left my heart faltering.
I weep for your journey, your path I had known,
Watching fishermen's craft at the river's edge.
This news isn't the long-awaited race's end,
You ventured to the land of goldfish, a fate to surpass.
Yet time's cooking fire didn't touch your share,
A girl who sought womanhood life's truths to announce.
You swam against tides embracing skills,
Becoming a mother, sister, a path rare to home.
But threnodies whispered your tales sideways,
Until the last key was struck, silence's song.
Time & Song of the River Man
I know you as of a girl who set out to see life's face,
Caught in marriage's masquerade facing strife.
A journey that embraced you to mother earth's breast,
Untimely you found your eternal rest. Adieu, rest in peace.

# Gift is Dead

This verse commences with a scene,
A water pot shattering a moment,
Upon memory's riverbank it unfolds,
Your name etched with dice stories.
Farewell, dear Ugochi, a somber refrain,
Once loved now turning to twice hated.
Your departure peaceful whispers truth,
Yet this death not life that stole your story.
August delivers news a mournful one -
Yet should the ocean return love shall prevail.
In the embrace of waves should you come again,
Dear gift, love's embers would never quench.

# For the Boys Who Left Home

(a requiem)

Daily I stroll through memory's lane,

Where owls' mournful chirps sing a requiem's strain.

The path winds past galloping hills high,

Steps pushed forward - yet at times held awry.

Crossing the river's divide I strive,

Yet unswimmable tides keep dreams animated.

Bars stand tall obstacles persist,

Pushing against a challenge to battle.

Unknown tales linger shaping the mode,

Tomorrow uncertain still I find my say.

This chap may lack promises of morrow,

For the Boys Who Left Home Early

Yet bitterness sipped sweetens time's grief.

Our present's time together may be fleeting,

But like fishermen fish will be caught.

A joyous end for those with fishing line,
Yet what fate befalls fish left behind?

# Funeral of Things We Lost

Amid the burial of dreams we mourn,

The preacher's words like balm were stomached.

Sermons of life after the last snort,

Amen whispered calming in its depth.

We anointed our wounded hearts raw and sore,

With "Amen" as if a cure, a remedy, a tradition.

A veiled guise to shield our broken state,

Concealing the fractures, love's heavy mass.

For when one falls, we all descend,

In death's grasp, unity won't twist.

So "Amen" we echo to soften the blow,

A shelter from the pain, a refuge we identify.

# Naming of Grief

This boy abridged to debris in the night,
Tries to grasp the fragments of his own luminous,
What remains of my journey's becoming?
This shard so fragile slipping from my embrace,
A name whispered as stories unfold,
Manhood, what transformation lies beneath?
The boy gazes upon his mirror's face,
Yet the glass murmurs of times' ignominy,
Becoming things that hold no true meaning.
As if those who came before believed it so,
Clung to ideals as they sailed life's stream,
Did they truly make it theirs, or just a borrowed glow?
As they swam across the shores of destiny's terrestrial,
Did their efforts shape destiny's hand,
Leaving behind a sign, a legacy's ghost?

# Realities of Our Being

Bare I arrive,
Clad as I depart,
Unto Mother Earth,
All is integral fragment.
To mortals, it's demise,
To spirits, a solemn vow,
Back to origin, the spirit flies,
Continuing the journey somehow.
Yet I stare at tombs so bare,
And at adornments squandered,
To Earth's embrace we shall repair,
Next steps, the spirit's vision pondered.
Who hides within the chamber's hold,
To outlive earthly clay and decay?

# Nameless

An emptiness resides deep within me,

When school's echo fades, what could it remain?

Memories of water flowing through my arrows,

A route traced from elusive, numbered strands.

Gatherings and knowledge's cost entwine,

As this house we've built guards tales of spell,

If it knew our trails, a history as survivors,

Our stories would bind us to life's endless brooks.

But above the water's name, a nation's due,

A land that sees its own as wanderers aflame,

A country that distances itself from history's eyes.

Last night a song and a gathering's buzz,

Fathers of our tales danced hearts cask,

To the rhythm of time's ever-turning wheel.

Within my walls, an emptiness does unfold,

To be uncounted is a fate forecast,

May I be remembered, even in netherworld's habitat,

As a life once lived, along life's snaking road.

# Things that Happened to Us

The preacher's voice proclaimed bold and wise
"Not all that gleams is gold to grasp."
As we shut our eyes blind to the theft
They snatched our light leaving us orphaned.
The beacon that guided our winding path
Needed time's touch to gather its force.
To glimmer as value's gems always do
Time's patient touch crafting the right.
But in their grasp it turned like birds in flight
They soared afar beyond our sight
To realms untamed far from where we've been.

# Sermon for the Once Loved

What can money purchase

For a son estranged

From his father's warm embrace?

Perhaps only the silhouettes and confines

Captured in family portraits,

Constraining affection and nurturing hostility.

Where the young ones imbibe

Deceptions veiled as paternal shadows,

But inquire within, for truth resides in no distant.

What transpires when love falters?

Resentment and confinement,

Against the once cherished, now twice reviled.

# When You Have None to Cheer You Up

Should I not embrace my mother's memories,
Or perhaps, the fleeting moments with my father?
This is a song not worthy of singing,
Though its verses are woven with fine lace and linings.
No, it is not.
How we stretched our wings like soaring birds,
For it is said: pursue your dreams,
In a world teeming with both fulfilled and unfulfilled hopes,
How else should one navigate the yearnings of the heart,
In a fractured portrait of a boy and blurred family tales?
The words advise: seek what you desire and live,
So, he stood on the shores of life, waving his hands,
Like the reeds along the banks of the Nile River,
Time & Song of the River Man
The river that brings tidings to the reeds,

Through seasons they tenderly thrive,

Dreams, ambitions, and the ascent to greatness.

In this realm called Earth, how does one persevere,

Where the very hands that once nurtured your dreams,

Now cast you down to the abyss of icy oceans,

Even in that portrait, you gasp for breath,

Seeking salvation in the language of ballads,

This is the genesis of betrayed birds that sing.

Holding untold tales of wishes and yearning to cheer,

But ultimately, they become mocking refrains of failures,

Where once there was whispered encouragement to take steps or
leaps,

Tell me, how does one survive solely on words,

Framed within the arsenal of their hearts,

Even when we know that words often betray their masters?

The note is struck, and suddenly, the music ceases,

Marking the beginning of another story where we are the birds,

Nesting alongside dirges and with broken wings and beaks,

No hands to provide our daily sustenance,

No hands to applaud our triumphs in flight school.

*The music is silenced, and the gathering disperses.*

# Is There No Time to Say Goodbyes?

Soar on the wings of these words,
Where mortality dons the cloak of immortality,
And verbiage mends the scars
Of epochs when zephyrs scoured away
Instances from the fabric of existence.
Love blossoms in every fervent embrace,
Time interlaces with you, intertwining with life.
I have inscribed you into these verses,
Hoping your journey culminates in paradise,
Once cherished, forever cherished in the great beyond.
If "farewell" must be the last word spoken,
Let time rewind, granting us another moment,
A parting in the hushed chambers of eternity,
From the warm embrace of cessation,
As the ember extinguishes without warning.

Time & Song of the River Man

*Death is but a comma in the story of this life.*

# Gin and Ship

Sunset hues grace the sky's vast arena,

A ship docked shadows of destiny rove,

Gin's bitter taste on the altar of words,

Greed and gain exchanged, like soaring natures.

A ship's hull laden with lives and wares,

A sailing vessel a journey that goads,

Yet beneath sails concealed by grief's blanket,

The history lost wrapped in another's shroud.

Through tongues that tell history dwindles,

Lost in the horizon where the sun cascade,

A ship sets sail bound for the strange,

In the realm of time's ebbing and grown.

# Our Tales

This tale's genesis lies along the shore,
In my homeland sea's reverence we esteem,
From the sea's bounty to its mysteries grand,
We worshiped gods and goddesses.
When the ships arrived, we ran to their embrace,
They bowed before thrones they sought,
Gins exchanged we carried the weight on our skins,
Becoming their burden altering fate.
Rivers and ships intertwined their course,
Whales devoured many natures' vigor,
Some became gods our destiny's strain,
As we embarked our homeland's dream.
Arriving on distant shores we realized,
Our tales originated where rivers met skies,
Mouth of the river the beginning site,
Our Tales Desert's edge where our stories grow wings.

# There is a Place Where I Belong

The wind carves its course clear,
Drought bows to its arrival season's cue.
Fire's path it scorches with valor,
Destroying all that hinders its flight.
Ant weaves its labyrinth unseen,
Winter's cold can't touch where it's stood.
Eagle's strength commands the breeze,
Wind dances to its authority with comfort.
Kites navigate their journeys well-timed,
Hen's survival mastered - life's model.
Rain knows its rhythm - dance it tells,
Iroko tree stands firm - a living art.
There is a Place Where I Belong
Harmattan arrives, the knowing few prepare,
Thick woods emerge, their strength they part.
When man falls, let him rise like kernels,

Planted anew, from adversity freed.

A place awaits where each fit,

Seek it, embrace it, where life throngs.

Find it, seek it, let your essence unfurl,

Live it, in full, let your life spin.

# How We Prayed Knowing Our Roots

We launched the canoe towards the western bank,

Yearning to glimpse our Savior's visage.

For they deemed us a people astray,

The river's face shimmered with liquid gold.

We knelt before the Savior's mother,

There, we prayed in a tongue unknown.

Hail to you, Mother Africa,

How sweet your breast milk upon our tongues.

We have convened to draw life from your form,

From every crevice of your body,

Life sprouts, adorning our world's beauty.

*But does my name still need to bleed for you?*

# History

History, when veiled in an unknown tongue,
Leaves you teetering on walls unrewarded,
Where even breath becomes a testament,
A metaphor for life's fierce evidence.
I know our stories, native tales so dear,
Before the shorelines, they echo pure,
Our waist's dance by riverside's flow,
Bringing fish to the nets, life's ebb and tide.
History, when another's lips reveal,
They omit how seashells our homes did lid,
A tale whispered by tides' coming and going,
A people entwined with the sea's rhythmic sinuous.
History, whether to ensnare or free,
Begins at the altar, unfolds to decree,
Binding or unbinding wills in chains,
Time & Song of the River Man
Saving from the river's maw's watery wheels.
Where survival resides, an overflow's tale,
A burden heavy, a color's moan,

History is the bridge that spans these coasts,
A narrative of struggles, triumphs, and more.

# Slavery

Always a melody when you are near,
Nightly your name's mention, hearts twinges,
They shatter your talons sink deep,
Bonds woven a connection to retain.
Upon my black skin traces unfold,
Signs of our union, a story ineffable,
Never the same since our first embrace,
Love's imprint left; time cannot erode.
Yet I yearn to break free from your clench,
Tear off the claws that entwine enclasp,
For in your hold while love's fire ignites,
Freedom beckons as day meets the dusks.

# Water Act

In this poem I trace the origin to water's flow,
It is where it begins or perhaps where it is meant.
They cast some into the water's squeeze,
Calmness unfolded a tranquil space,
Yet beneath it masked a treacherous move,
Deception cloaked in the stillness to object.
When thoughts of home arise, we may show novelty.
From waterways' outlook our views confined,
In shame we bury our heads hiding,
The truths hidden in waters' see-through.
The water once believed a friend,
Betrayed us with painted lies in vibrant hue,
But beneath the surface intentions divulge,
A facade that stories of the waters veil.

# The Lad and the River

This tale unfolds from the boundless ocean,

A narrative of worth denied a decree,

Like stories of black-skinned fellas,

Whose lives on ship decks were stories voiced,

Destined to the Badland their fates cast.

Pity he shall not garner from the vast ocean,

If whales get hungry, they feast with no excitement,

The weak they devour, feeding history's lore,

And if labor is his want, then let him be,

Recall numbers, 15, 20, 22, they tell,

A language where his fate rings a mournful sound.

A word pinned to the family's wall,

You're the water flooding my parched lands,

Every thought, an island's river's flow,

Overwhelms my thatched dwelling,

Where every owl's cry is a song of loss,

Time & Song of the River Man

Not just tremors, but threnodies athwart.

If these tales cease not, let me know the time,

Wake me from dreams of fatherhood's hike,

The lad by the river's edge waves to his dreams,

Dreams like waves, flowing in rhythmic torrents,

But waves never leave, dreams are not at ease,

For the man in his peace, dreams the ocean's end.

# Sowing Time

How do you sow seeds that won't sprout?
As the preacher's words tumble from his lips,
Into the fertile earth and our tear-filled eyes.
Hearts torn by storms, revealing our fragility,
We are seeds meant for planting, but we won't grow
From where we are sown, our destiny unknown.
Thus, the gathering of these seeds, humankind,
Sown in seasons and times, whether fair or foul,
Man must be sown into the soil, becoming memories.
*How do you plant what refuses to burgeon?*

# The Place of Gods

The veil parts, revealing
the truth's cascade,
A Ray's silhouette, unbri-
dled, defiant.
Upon ebony canvas, a
mark takes hold,
A question etched, in in-
trospection's gold-leaf.
A query posed to heavens
high,
And to ebony realms
where spirits fib.
It challenges the earth's
expanse,
It challenges souls in a cos-
mic ballet.
Are gods mere harbingers
of fate's cruel face,
No mention of them in

kindness' loveliness?
In whispered echoes, their
stories dwindle,
She succumbed to their
ailment, their dark cru-
sade.

# About Last Night

In the night's embrace, my
fingers trace the lunation,
Though moonless, dark-
ness cradles whispers of
boon,
A tranquil peace that the
shadows bequeath,
As our hands intertwine, a
bond aglow.
In the depths of the dark,
hearts shine so cheerful,
Illuminating fears that
once took flight,
Tongues unite, kissing
worries away,
Easing the burdens of each
passing diurnal.

That night, love's birds
nested, side by side,
Love born anew whisper-
ing peace,
Nightingale's songs sere-
nade their hearts' core,
"I love you" echoes eter-
nally.
First kisses exchanged, true
love takes trip,
The night chimes beckon-
ing futures in sight,
Amid the storms of lost
love's wind,
Time & Song of the River
Man
Reminiscent night, their
love sets sail.
Love once lost, rediscov-
ered its domain,
Two souls together, love's
flames rekindled,
Moonlit skies witness their
perfect embrace,
As "amen" echoes, love's
promise they air.

# Watching the River Flow

Tonight, I shall immerse
myself once again,
In this ocean's waves, its
relentless roar,
For loving you has sub-
merged me deep,
In its currents, secrets that
my heart preserves.
A ritual repeated as each
day cracks open,
Dipping my heart as the
river churns,
For rivers flow stones they
may eat away at,
Yet who is to know where
pain's rivers flow?

Might they wash away the
fragments of me,
My broken pieces cast out
to the sea,
As I stand here observing
the rivers' course,
Seeking solace, tracking
the flow's vigor.
Here I stand to witness to
grasp,
Where waters clash stones
their battle send,
And I linger to witness
love's journey too,
Time & Song of the River
Man
To witness what loving
you can untie.

# Motherhood

Motherhood, a crown
upon my head it lay.
Anchoring my navel cord's
sacred habits,
The crown of humanity,
shared by wholly,
A lane of life, where foot-
steps fall.
Haven of solace, where life
seeks to fleece,
Fertile land of growth
where dreams reside,
Joyous essence in life's
journey's scheme,
Home's builder weaving
love's layer.
Motherhood - the title

worn by sundry.
Co-creator with God life's
symphony,
A still voice in attentive
ear's hold,
Wisdom's whisper more
precious than gilt.

# Conversation with the Ghost of My Mother After My Wife Left Home Why Our Kids

It began so with a subtle drowsy song,

To the sacred altar of motherhood's thrall.

A once radiant sun obscured by veils,

And my eyes wept on many night's paths.

She glimpsed a boy's fragments - torrents -

Raging waters, trials in disarray,

They held the weight of the journeying pedes,

Yet she comprehended my struggle's beat.

She knows the cracked edge of city's hedge,

A portrait of me, broken, in its sprawl,

Mother's touch brought tranquility's tide,

Down my brow soothing like moon's glow.

Conversation with the Ghost of My Mother

After My Wife Left...

Through quiet time my heart's desires spill,

Longing for a mother's warmth,

She shared tales of a grieving wife,

And broken lad's offspring embracing dirge.

They wandered seeking solace, a release,

From father's words, a language not at unity,

The children loved - though his speech was fading,

Bound by the constraints that time had voiced.

# Marriage 1

Upon your altar my breath's last sigh.

Yet a voice within me stirs and yells,

"Awake! This isn't the end,

Your journey continues paths unclear."

Nights pledge tranquility's sweet grip,

But echoes at home flee without a trace.

Shall you depart, never to return?

Maybe ancient times, we'd ache.

The past might have worn a gentler look,

Nostalgia's haze, a comforting space.

Yet onward we tread our lives reveal,

New tales, new chapters, in stories untold.

# Marriage 2

Marriage, a reservoir of ache deep,

You've shattered walls within my ground.

I lay exposed surrendering all,

My desires yield to memories,

Yet you stand firm unyielding,

A fortress of the past, stories untold.

Last night you held the lad in your grasp,

Innocence unaware of deceit's tight clows,

Cries of anguish and despair,

A symphony of agony the heart's dress.

# Titillation (Don't Blame Me)

I honor you my woman,
Your body is now my sa-
cred shrine,
Where worship's essence
softly falls,
Upon pleasure's altar
within your parapets.
In the garden of love's ce-
lestial compass,
Seeds of generations we
plant here,
I approach you now, my
heart aglow,
Guided by passion's river's
current.
Where liberty and life in-

terweave,
Two pillars strong, a wel-
come you regard,
Transforming a wandering
soul's fate,
Into a realm of love's park-
land.
I hail you, my woman,
with utmost beauty,
Planting seeds of love in
this tranquil space,
Open the gate, let our
journey begin,
Titillation (Don't Blame
Me)
With hands on pillars, my
reverence immense.
May your land receive my
shepherd's staff,
A symbol of generations,
harmony awed,
May our love be as alluvial
soil,
Bearing life's fruit with joy
and labor.
Amen to this union, this
sacred bond,
Where love and life to-
gether re-join.

# My Woman

My woman stands as the
final pace,
Droplets of water, my
thirst's guide,
As the sun parches, she's
my relief,
Quenching my throat's
yearning, a credence.
On rainy nights, her hands
embrace,
My naked form, love's sa-
cred park,
Morning's harsh breath,
she tempers well,
Fanning my fires, stories to
express.
Lost soul, they say, but

how can that be,
When in her embrace, I'm
truly welcome.
Her thighs are the trails,
leading to harmony,
Apples of salvation, life's
sweet ensuance.
She's the lace that veils
passion's deep ocean,
A haven where I resurface,
love's plea,
When life's tempests assail
heart and depth,
My Woman
She empowers, making me
whole.
In her grace, I find strength
again,
My woman, my love, for-
ever true.

# A Requiem

Within me a tree takes root deep,

Its whisper bears my name a familiar sound.

Twenty, then twenty-one it chimes anew,

Yet with an unfamiliar voice, it bred.

With time, it adopts the word "father",

Oh, dear boy child, may your life imbue.

This is not mere poetry, but a heartfelt tale,

A narrative woven with emotions that conquer.

# First Night in the City of My Father

Upon that inaugural eve with you
Amidst the whispered wish that you grace
This ancestral soil, your native hearth
Envisioned serenity was my tranquil thought
As your mother, called by cleansing waters, withdrew
While I beheld your gesticulating fingers' dance
The murmur I perceived as you lay abed -
Oh, my yearning to converse with you
In sequestered dialogue, directed at your liquid gaze
The very tenor of your milky wails
Summoned your mother in hastened flurry
To fathom where my unintended vigor had alighted
Yet, comprehend, it was no harsh contact I rendered
Still, your wordless infant tongue failed to attest
As your cries, prolonged and resonant, filled the air -
They invoked a paternal craving, a plea to nurture
As night surrendered to the advancing day

Through urban landscapes, our voyage unfurled

In pursuit of the enigma behind your tears' cascade

In the metropolis of your paternal lineage, together we ventured

Only to unveil the truth: this odyssey was destined to be protracted

# For My Son (Sobeife)

I have engaged in an intimate dance with time upon this reflective surface,
Witnessing myself as a portrayal within fate's grasp,
Each passing moment, I cleanse away the faint smudges,
Those traces of life that blemish the construct called man.
I bear in mind that my home lies a decade hence,
If this younger self learns solely from a fractured mirror,
One that endeavors to capture the semblance of a lineage,
Where words cascade like snow, gentle yet deafening.
The sweetness of existence permeates through the avenues,
Words, like tempests, are hailed and resound mightily,
In the silence left by speech and soundless echoes,
What shape does the heart take? What of legacy?
Termed a child, and children forming a familial tableau,
Should we once more stand before the mirror's gaze,
And should the bell toll, "*gbim, gbim, gbim,*" in chorus,
This resonance too reverberates as a call from our origins.

Not a composition of verse, refrain not from joining,

In a symphony of prose, your sentiments found their path.

# Heaven is Not Safe

In the presence of these resounding walls,
Adorned by the spectrum of human hues
These pigments sculpt our souls,
From the somber shadows to velvety browns,
The canvas radiates, yet some forms recede,
Dwelling as mere contours and silhouettes,
Birthing anew with the ink of another,
This artist crafts bodies mirroring bodies,
A reflection of the exterior made material.
But, at the center, divinity whispers,
Here lies paradise, yet skepticism persists,
For within these gatherings, disparities bloom,
Unleashing tidal currents that sunder rather than unite,
Labeled heaven, yet harboring rifts in human fabric,
A realm where dissonances echo in bilabial symphony,
Moistening what disjoins, more than what binds.
Time & Song of the River Man
Termed heaven, but our hearts carry plunder,
Seeking refuge in crusades of division,
A cycle etched and labeled divine,

Where icy detachment becomes a divine decree,

At the altar, the butchery of our shared humanity,

And paradoxically, this very essence reunites us.

In this ethereal realm, a haven you inhabit,

Pray, recount your journey through the night,

Those heralding the dawn's illumination,

As we stood witness, observing our creations,

The canvas of our gatherings and souls,

Brought to life by the dexterity of our hands.

Tell me, does this haven stand secure for us?

Or does paradise remain treacherous terrain for mortals?

Indeed, paradise must harbor dangers yet unveiled,

For human nature itself renders its safety uncertain.

# Is God a Poet (Joel)

In the beginning, God crafted the light of day,
Out of an expanse once void and bare,
For the delight of our discerning eyes to behold.
So, tell me, how does one weave a poem's essence,
If not by the union of alphabets and syllables,
From the repository of metaphors, plucking verses,
Lyrics that unfurl, grasped by the eyes of the heart.
In this narrative, even God takes on the form of poetry,
A creation within the poet's realm,
Seeking to render the unseen visible,
Bridging the chasm between the tangible and ethereal.
God fashions beings, both male and female, for allegory,
To stand as guides, pointing towards heart's yearnings,
They roam through the garden, christening existence,
Assigning names to all they perceive, thus forming
Animals, objects, humans, and their counterparts.
And then, God concludes creation, a day defined as rest.
If God, too, isn't a poet, then what truly is the essence of poetry?

# Sermon One

Oh, sacred muse, descend and grace us,

Where the world once ensnared us in its grasp,

We yearn to infuse existence with vitality,

If not today, then let me immerse within your essence,

To ascend from this slumber of decades and muse,

Myself and my name into the tapestry of future history.

I ache to stand there and unveil the veracity,

Life as a wordsmith, sculpting destiny's narrative,


Muse, heed the call and inspire once more.

# Begging Brother

I kneel a ladder aspiring,
Toward heavens' realm, dreams embryonic,
Wouldn't you rejoice,
To ascend where celestial voices are singing?
If I plead seeking your past's lore,
To understand the pathways you once yawn,
Do I now possess,
The wealth of ages your story's tact?

# Painter

The world a void vast and unadorned,
A canvas unfamiliar to brown skin's glare,
Another arrived his world to paint anew,
Brushstrokes of cruelty brutality's sort.
He sat upon ship's deck silent and meek,
A sheep shipped voiceless lost and frail,
Their books' words seeped deep indoors,
Brown skin feeding his world's dark debauchery.
Nights yearned for nostalgia's tender embrace,
Yet home lay wasted, trust's fall from beauty,
Buried between images untrue I bore, Lost in the painted illusions love constrained.
Unable to find myself nor home's arrival,
In the void my essence seemed to churn,
But know this, beneath the world's cruel roof,
Your identity thrives, your heart is home – Africa.

# Songs

Upon my tongue, there dwell inscribed sorrows,

Nestled amid every melody's embrace,

Interlacing tangs of bitterness and nectar's grace,

Yet, a lexicon eludes me to articulate their presence.

Before the tribunal of a world that scrutinizes,

We're assessed by the words we summon,

Entreating them to heed our harmonies,

Or heedlessly discard them to oblivion's abyss.

*Does melody serve as a vantage to perceive life's vesture?*

The ballad persists, an unending cadence, an utterance of p a i n,

Within these verses I intone,

For I've mastered their tune, their rhythm,

A solace woven to soothe my heart's lament.

Thus, I seek solace in melodies sublime,

Whether verbal or couched in brevity, For it's said that music wields
the power to mend,

To mend even the fractures etched in fragile hearts.

# Broken Muse

I have departed from the bay,
Her words still echoing, seeking self-care.
"Do not trace my steps this time,
This journey has no return."
I wander along the riverside,
Perhaps seeking the right words,
To mend this somber heart,
For loving shadows has bruised it.
A pulse, a yearning for the sea,
Take a journey back to the source,
We inhale the waters and swallow our tears,
Questioning why this path is rugged.
Whispers echo within the shadows,
Let words mend the eager hearts,
And love those untouched by pain,
The voyage commences with a thrust,
Take serenity with you into the world.

# Season of Songs

A song imprisoned on my tongue it stays,
No key to unlock its lyrical labyrinth,
Deep within my core, the words abide,
Yet my tongue yearns to let them jaunt.
My heart beats a decade's timeless beat,
Searching for ears, melodies to flood,
Where love, like crime, in metaphors bargains,
Words hiding scars, heart's subtle bind.
Drenched birds lack melodies of cheer,
Shattered mirrors, beauty evaporates,
Water splashes fail to touch the soul,
Value wanes against annoyance's ring.
A history broken, sun's rays elude,
Fear-drowned voices remain silent,
Bound severed, connections no longer hold,
A water pot shattered; stories ineffable.

# Surge

What words did they utter branding as sins?
Calabash shattered at stream's mouth.
Close by, yet beyond grasp my self-slip-ups,
Like water's droplet, as time's current clutches.
My tongue like water, flowed in its duel,
Words spilled soaking my land's embrace,
Flooded the humble thatch where I declare,
Ideals and dreams woven with mending.

# Singing Distance

Every evening of my odyssey,

I revisit this arid expanse,

Planting a solitary blossom for you—

A name from my lips,

A name I alone can truly utter,

With an intimacy that surpasses all others.

In this parched terrain where I sow,

I have gleaned the art of coaxing blooms,

Guiding them toward the light—

To savor that inaugural sunrise,

I bathe them in each tear,

Those that cascade from my eyes,

A tribute to ensure your memory never fades.

# Stitching Memories

Upon the pathways where memories have bid farewell,
With each step as our hearts intertwine with the unfolding road,
Conversing with the soul of time and seasons dressed in crimson,
Our hearts yearn to mend the spaces between.
These verses serve as our guide, tracing the footsteps,
Shimmering over a distant horizon adorned with joy,
Where dreams, like patchwork quilts, stand ready,
As free as each drop of rain from the heavens.

# Orchestra of Existence

At the lad's funeral, solemn and still,

They preached sermons on life's resilience,

Yet the lad, in peace, chose not to return.

For my people believe, unwavering,

That should one's life's purpose remain unfulfilled,

They shall be reborn, time and again, to seek it.

But as the congregation mourned and believed,

I gazed upon the sky through their tear-filled eyes,

And in their sorrow, the lad found his heaven,

Knowing he had accomplished his earthly tasks.

Amidst their cries for him to return,

To care for his aging parents, nearing their end,

The lad, in bliss, understood not their belief,

That the young must bear the weight of the old.

# Staring at Self in a Portrait of Time

In the cocoon of time, a prophecy lies,

This child, a chrysalis of dreams,

Shall metamorphose into a butterfly of prayer,

Engaging in battles both inner and unseen.

Within the fortress of the heart, wars unfurl,

A choice to conquer or to yield to fear,

The boy-soldier evolves, strides towards manhood,

Spanning the arc of moonlight and endless nights.

Amidst the dark and the daunting,

All that seeks to intimidate,

Resides an indomitable essence within him,

The very essence of a man's creation.

Persistently, he returns, capturing moments in frames,

A visual testament to the transience of existence,

In the lens of time's camera, treasures dissolve,

Yet, they linger as echoes of resplendent dew,

Behold, the blossoming of everything wondrous,

An iridescence akin to glistening moisture,

He stands unwavering, gazing at the nexus of tomorrow and now,

A portrait painted with anticipation and hope.

This canvas shall converse through the medium of waters,

Should it not be erased by the tides of change,

Today, as the boy unfurls into manhood's embrace, The tapestry of

becoming, woven with beauty,

Shall etch its tale upon the tapestry of existence.

# Time and Songs

Countless prayers have graced this ground,

Desires suspended on life's ebbing tides,

Sequential footsteps mark transitions,

From childhood through the voyage of adulthood,

Now poised on the precipice of manhood's expanse.

Through epochs, aspirations and reveries flowed,

Here, I've returned to gather them methodically,

Gently collecting each fragment, one by one,

Until my basket overflows with hopes anew.

A life encapsulated in the present, in continuance,

This juncture, this moment in the circuit,

Unique in its fleeting emergence,

Yet, over time, I've thrived,

Living within this instance, within this day,

For in this symphony of existence,

We were once borne upon the shores by the tide, Whether today or the morrow, time's whims will decide.

# Song One

*very funny to admit, but all life still clings to a song*

   -Ifeanyi Prosper

The bustling road murmurs to me,

A tale of fatherhood.

My heir grows up, far away,

Unacquainted with his roots.

As the melodies linger,

I strain my ears,

Anticipating the proclamation.

I, a wanderer,

Pursuing a destiny,

I, once confronted with a choice: "Pick me or the books,"

Stacked on countless shelves,

An unfamiliar love.

There, I surrendered my life,

In pursuit of finding it,

The initial and subsequent rains,

Drenched my aspirations,

Where I stand now,

Love and life have intertwined,

Branding me the trailing tale,

Laying siege to a fortress.

# The First Time I Singed

Ever since Mother heralded Father's arrival,
I have mastered the art of anticipation to meet him.
The man she would prostrate before, imploring,
*Don't emulate his absence from home.*
Some narratives need not pass through a mother's lips,
For her, it's another path to redemption.
She would stand at the window, supplicating,
*O birds of the sky, return with tidings of him.*
He had tarried and wandered for decades now,
This was the deluge that soaked my youth.
That night he unveiled his heart, whispering love,
I believed, becoming an ardent disciple of love.
The harmattan breeze sent shivers through me,
As I gazed into his eyes, I understood the essence of love.

# We all Sing

A boy perched on the world's edge,
Voicing the grief that dwells within,
Of a homeland marred by gloom,
Its cries echo tangled in the air.
Nigeria, a land fraught with strife,
Built upon ruins,
In the blood of her own, she's made,
A tale of pain, unceasingly retold.
Each call for freedom meets bullets' bite,
In courts, justice veers from its rightful hoop,
Our course distorted, intentions defied,
For gains unrighteous, where life is cut off.
For no one is immortal, all shall kiss the dust,
While the earth endures, a timeless core,
As voices rise, young and old, in pain,
We all Sing Seeking a future where hope shall endure.

# After a Birth

Not garbed in silver or gold are my words,
Amidst this debris where time intertwines with us,
Yet, if language stitches hearts and spirits,
Let my ink flow, stark in black and white.
Within this hush, a sanctuary is discovered,
Wherein we coexist, interlacing our trails,
With verbiage that soothes the desolate,
A landscape akin to the fields of Springfield and *Bhulaland*.
Peace, oh peace, let it resound in echo,
As words slip through the window's threshold,
Into the chambers of thought within our minds,
And through the avenues beyond spoken sound.
Without them, unity dissolves into tranquility,
Thus, let words cascade within our metaphorical garden,
Cultivating awareness of the paths we've traversed,
After a Birth
In soft whispers, "I recognize you, once in a lifetime."
Grateful for your birthday blessings,
May these words be a vessel of gratitude in return.

# Sowing Time

How can one sow what refuses to burgeon?

As the preacher's utterances cascade,

Landing upon the receptive soil and our brimming gaze.

Within the chambers of our hearts, tempests brew,

Revealing our vulnerability as nature's testament,

Yet, our essence resists sprouting where we're sown.

Thus unfolds the assembly of these potential seeds,

Human, enigmatic fruits bound for sowing,

Within seasons and epochs, benevolent or harsh.

Man, destined to be sown into the earth's embrace,

Shall sprout naught but through the fertile soil of memory,

How then does one implant the ungerminative?

*Is it not to understand that growth transcends mere earth?*

# Time

You have laid ambush to cut me down -

I, a sojourner of life

In every portrait,

Where I stared at Time cuts my wings

To fly home -

I nest within memories

While the wind cracks to take me home

Work and time keep hailing On me, the brimstones of appetite

Of a home within the offspring of my school

Here, I, a sojourner lay -

Time cuts my wings to fly home to nurse self

In a portrait of a man seeking

To grasp life with bare hands-on

The axe head must turn to its owner

So, the portrait with time will come again

Time & Song of the River Man

With wings, memories, and the now.

# Good Night

My people hold the belief steadfast,

That if one's life's purpose goes unfulfilled, They shall return, time and again, to seek it.

Thus, we raise our hands to the skies,

Beseeching for the return of our cherished soul,

The one we've just laid to rest today.

Yet the heavens answer with rainfall,

A reminder that we have strayed from our path.

# Self at the 33rd Bridge

*Dear self,*

Numerous lessons I have gathered to wield,

At this crossroads of the thirty-third degree,

Where the Earth once met its savior,

And he treads the same path and years.

Life, history, and the unfurling future held him high. Today, I, a

wanderer on the sands of an hourglass,

Measure life's essence with every tick.

I have learned that all birds have their perches,

Even when their names escape the tongue's grasp.

I have learned that birds sing in the rain,

Unperturbed by the cold hands that hold them.

Even though it is said that birds of a feather

Flock together, strengthening their nests,

Self at the 33rd Bridge

I, a wanderer, have learned that one such bird,

Here and now, is worth far more than ten thousand,

Those eluding our grasp, beyond our reckoning.

It is said that not all that gleams is gold,

For those who seek it might stumble.

At this threshold, I cling to faith and fate,

Conducting the course of the river that carries me.

If time were my constant companion,

I, the nomad, fleeing my yesterdays,

The youth, whose glory I prod but do not boast of,

This too I have embraced and consoled my heart,

While I stand gazing at the horizon and what life may bring.

But for the journey of this life I traverse,

I race to meet a destiny where it shall embrace

My toil with tender lips, ushering in the dreams I have yearned for,

As I, who have toiled and waited, hope life's lessons

Will converge where I will dwell eternally.

# Two-Timing

Some days my mirror betrays me,
Reflecting a man with smiles it weaves,
Concealing fears that dwell within,
Tremors that love's whispers initiate.
Fears alight on each word of affection,
Love's call a tremor, a poignant fitting together,
The tremor, it shatters, breaks the heart,
Tearing the soul, tearing it at a distance.
Some days, my mirror fabricates illusions,
Portraying perfection before my eyes,
A self it claims is an image ideal,
Yet beneath the truth it conceals, inhabits me.

# Hope

I grasp the sea my love, in my embrace,
Where the shore murmurs secrets,
A haven of strength - resilience's call,
Whispering fortitude, a shelter for just.
I swim through the waves seeking the slurp,
Tied by fate to ocean's future, a heave,
Despite the dredging challenges that upsurge,
I persist, surmounting towards the skies.
In every line etched upon my hand's expanse,
I've named existence, life's intricate ballet,
Palms holding wisdom's hallowed rituals,
Casting shadows that foretell destiny's state.
As the horizon unfolds its canvas eclectic,
Dreams alight on safe wings they glide,
Landing softly, melding with what's to stay,
Hope In this dance of life, aspirations set free.

# About the Author

**JohnChinakaOnyeche** is a multi-talented individual, wearing the hats of an author, poet, and educator specializing in History and African History. He boasts an impressive literary repertoire that includes works such as *"Echoes Across The Atlantic, A Night Tale At The Threshold Of Howl, We Returned To Kiss The Cross,*

*The Broken Fort, A Good Day For Tomorrow's Coming, Stateless,*

*25 Atonements, The Morning Came Calling Our Names,"* and *"The Gathering Of Reeds,"* scheduled for publication in March 2024 by Ethel Zine Press. Additionally, he has crafted a chapbook titled "Chapters of Broken Tales." John's literary prowess has earned him recognition as a Best of Net Nominee.

Beyond his literary pursuits, John is a devoted husband and a loving father to two charming children, Sobeife and Chisimdiri. He hails from Igbodo, Etche, Rivers State of Nigeria and primarily creates his works in the vibrant city of Port Harcourt, Rivers State. While crafting his poetic and literary pieces, he draws inspiration from his academic background as a graduate of History and Diplomatic Studies at Ignatius Ajuru University of Education in Port Harcourt, Rivers State.

When he's not engaged in the creative process, John indulges in his passion for reading. To connect with this prolific writer and poet, you can reach out to him through various channels, including his blog at rememberajc.wordpress.com, Facebook at facebook.com/jehovahisgood, Twitter at twitter.com/apostlejohnchin, and email at apostlejohnchinaka@gmail.com. Additionally, you can explore more of his work and profiles through his linktree at https://linktr.ee/Rememberajc.

**You can connect with me on:**


**https://linktr.ee/Rememberajc**

www.ingramcontent.com/pod-product-compliance
Lightning Source LLC
Chambersburg PA
CBHW071541150726
48000CB00002B/887